365 AWESOME RANDOM USELESS FACTS

AMAZE & ANNOY OTHERS WITH AWESOME USELESS KNOWLEDGE

A Year's Worth of Random Useless Facts!

This book belongs to

\-.

Knowledge is power...but USELESS KNOWLEDGE HAS SUPERPOWERS!!

Amaze! Surprise! Entertain!
Annoy! Improve creativity!
Start conversation!

Inside this book is a random useless fact for every day of the year, though once you start reading you may find it hard to stop. Be prepared for your mind to want to gobble the contents of this book!

Find out which country does not have mosquitoes, the number of muscles in a caterpillar, which city has its own ant, where to find the longest staircase in the world, how much power your brain uses when it is thinking, and much more.

You may find it hard to keep these incredible useless facts to yourself. Don't! Start sharing your random useless knowledge whenever you can.

USELESS KNOWLEDGE HAS SUPERPOWERS -
a simple random useless fact can amaze, surprise, entertain, annoy, improve creativity, solve a problem, and start a conversation that could turn into a great friendship.

It is better to have useless knowledge that to know nothing.

Seneca the Younger

1.

The average person falls asleep in 7 minutes

2.

It is impossible for most people

to lick their own elbow.

3.

A crocodile cannot stick its tongue out.

4.

A shrimp's heart is in its head

5.

One of the toughest tongue twisters in the

English language is

"the sixth six sheiks sixth sheep's sick."

6.

Nine body parts as unique as your fingerprint are your iris, retina, ear shape, lip print, tongue, voice, toe print, teeth, your walk.

7.

A shark is the only fish that can blink with both eyes.

8.

Sea otters hold hands when they sleep. It keeps them from floating away from each other.

9.

Only 10-12 % of the population is left-handed.

10.

The dangly thing in the back of your throat is called a uvula.

11.

A cat has 32 muscles in each ear.

12.

Every time you lick a stamp you consume 1/10 of a calorie.

13.

Bees are found on every continent except for Antarctica.

14.

Caterpillars have 12 eyes.

15.

Slugs have four noses.

16.

Most insects hatch from eggs.

17.

The closest living relatives of Tyrannosaurus Rex are chickens and ostriches.

18.

An average yawn lasts six seconds.

19.

Kangaroos and Emu's can't walk backwards.

20.

Emu's are the only bird species that have calf muscles.

21.

The word 'four' has 4 letters

22.

Every dog's nose is unique, like a fingerprint.

23.

Frogs drink water through their skin.

24.

Owls don't have eyeballs.

Their eyes are more like tubes held rigidly in

place by bones.

That means they can't roll their eyes.

25.

In the Australian Daintree Rainforest there is a tree

with the common name Idiot Fruit. It is one of the

oldest flowering plants on the planet.

26.

A group of frogs is called an army.

27.

Humans share 50% of their DNA
with a banana.

28.

There are 31,557,600 seconds
in a year.

29.

A hippopotamus can run faster than a human.

30.

The human heart beats around

115,000 times a day.

31.

Ketchup used to be sold as a medicine.

It was thought to be a cure for indigestion.

32.

Your nose gets warmer when you lie.

33.

Some fish can cough.

They cough to clear particles and bacteria

out of their gills.

34.

Hawaiian pizza was invented in Canada.

35.

It takes on average 50 licks

to finish one scoop of ice cream.

36.

Play-doh was originally used as wallpaper cleaner.

37.

The Rubik's cube has 43,252,003,274,489, 856,000 color configurations and only one solution.

38.

The opposite sides of a die will always add up to 7.

39.

Strawberries are the only fruit that have seeds on the outside.

40.

Peanuts are not nuts, they are legumes.

41.

Ice Cream was once called 'cream ice'.

42.

It takes 2-3 years for a pineapple to grow full size.

43.

No number between 1-999 includes the letter 'a'

in it's word from. You won't find the letter 'a'

used until you hit one thousand.

44.

Playing dance music helps

ward off mosquitoes.

They don't like the frequency or

pitch of the music.

45.

In a deck of cards the King of Hearts
is the only king without a moustache.

46.

Dreamt is the only word in the English language that ends in mt.

47.

A group of hippos is called a bloat.

48.

Pogonophobia is a fear of beards.

49.

'A jiffy' is one trillionth of a second.

50.

Nearly all of a dragonfly's head is eye. They can see almost every angle except right behind them.

51.

Golf balls have anywhere between 300 -500 dimples. Most have 336.

52.

Ripe cranberries will bounce like a ball.

53.

Eating too many carrots could turn your skin orange.

54.

A group of porcupines is called a prickle.

55.

Finland has more sauna than cars.

56.

In Switzerland it is illegal to own only one guinea pig because they crave social interaction.

57.

You are taller in the morning than at night.

58.

Dolphins sleep with one eye open.

59.

Humans are the only animal on earth

to have chins.

No one knows why.

60.

Bananas are curved because they grow

towards the sun.

The process is called 'negative geo-tropism'.

61.

The average person produces roughly

30mls of saliva every hour.

If you live to be 72 you will have produced

enough saliva in your lifetime to fill 50 bathtubs.

62.

The smallest bone in your body is in your ear.

It is called the stapes bone.

63.

Most people fart between 14-23 times a day.

64.

St Lucia is the only country to be
named after a woman.

65.

The national animal of Scotland is the Unicorn.

66.

Zero is an even number.

67.

Sea lions have rhythm.

They are the only animal

that can clap to a beat.

68.

Your brain uses approximately 10 watts of energy to think.

69.

Hippopotamus milk is pink.

70.

Your fingernails grow faster when you are cold.

71.

No word in the English language rhymes with month, orange or silver.

72.

The average person spends six months of their life sitting at red lights waiting for them to turn green.

73.

The full name of the doll Barbie is Barbara Millicent Roberts

74.

The dot over the letter i is called a 'tittle'.

75.

Clouds look white because they are reflecting sunlight from above them.

76.

A bolt of lightning is five times hotter than the sun.

77.

Wind is silent until it blows against something.

78.

Yuma, Arizona gets on average 4000 hours of sunshine a year making it the sunniest place on earth.

79.

It is impossible to hum while holding your nose.

80.

The written word for every single odd number has an 'e' in it.

81.

A group of Lemurs is called a conspiracy.

82.

Wombat poo is cube shaped.

83.

Goats have rectangular pupils in their eyes.

84.

The Alaskan Wood Frog can hold its pee for up to eight months.

85.

You loose up to 30% of your taste buds during an aeroplane flight.

86.

Octopus blood is blue because it is copper based.

87.

Human blood is red because it is iron based.

88.

The lint that collects in the bottom of your pockets is called 'gnurr'.

89.

A snail can sleep for 3 years.

90.

Researchers say you can fool your mind into thinking you are happy and smiling if you put a pencil between your teeth.

91.

Tigers have striped skin not just striped fur.

92.

If you yelled for 8 years, 7months and 6 days you would have produced enough sound energy to heat one cup of coffee.

93.

A flea can jump 350 times it's body length. That is like a human being able to jump the length of a football field.

94.

Butterflies taste with their feet.

95.

An ostrich's eyes are bigger than it's brain.

96.

A chef's hat is called a toque.

It contains 100 folds.

97.

'E' is the most common letter in the English language.

E appears in 11% of all English words.

98.

Tornadoes used to be called 'twirl blasts'

& 'twirl winds' in the 18th century.

99.

Sharks existed on earth before trees.

Sharks have existed for around 400 million years,

trees for around 350 million.

100.

Umbrellas were once only used by women.

101.

Sloths have more neck bones than giraffes.

A giraffe has 7 vertebrae. A sloth has 10.

102.

Pigeon poop was once used to make gunpowder.

103.

Pharaoh Ramses IV of Ancient Egypt

had his eyes replaced with small onions

when he was mummified.

104.

By raising your legs slowly and lying on your back

you cannot sink into quicksand.

105.

The United States of America

Declaration of Independence

was written on hemp paper.

106.

Triskaidekaphobia means the fear of number 13.

107.

Camels have 3 eyelids.

108.

Half of all bank robberies

take place on a Friday.

109.

There are more chickens than people in the world.

110.

A rainbow can only be seen
in the morning or late afternoon.
A rainbow occurs when the sun is
40 degrees or less above the horizon.

111.

The plastic thing on the end of shoelaces
are called aglets.

112.

Bees have 5 eyes.
3 small eyes on the top of the head
and 2 larger ones in the front.

113.

The average bolt of lightening contains enough
energy to toast 100,000 pieces of bread.

114.

Ants closely resemble human mannerisms
when they start their day.
When they wake they stretch, appear to yawn,
then begin to start work.

115.

According to astronauts' space smells like
a combination of diesel fuel and barbecue.

116.

The smell in space is caused by dying stars.

117.

Taking just one step uses over
200 muscles in the body.

118.

The average person will spend a total of

3680 hours or 153 days

of their life searching for misplaced items.

119.

Talking to yourself makes your brain

work more effectively.

120.

Wild elephants only sleep for 2 hours a night.

121.

A jellyfish is 95% water.

122.

The Empire State Building has 1,860 stairs

to the 102 floor observatory.

123.

There are 1,792 steps in the Eiffel Tower.

124.

The longest staircase in the world
can be found on Niesen Mountain Switzerland
with 11,674 steps.

125.

When a Donkey and a Zebra have a baby
it's called a Zonkey.

126.

The smell of an orange can relieve stress.

127.

Mount Everest weighs an estimated
357 trillion pounds.

128.

The pupil in your eye expands up to 45%

when you look at someone you love.

129.

On average people have 100,000
hairs on their head.

130.

You can lose around 50-100 hairs a day.

131.

The LEGO factory produces around

36,000 pieces of Lego every minute.

132.

At Lego headquarters they have a vault

with a collection of every Lego

set they have made.

133.

In a room of 23 people there is a 50% chance

that two people will have the same birthday.

134.

"Forty" is the only number that is spelt with letters arranged in alphabetical order.

135.

Most people burp between 6-20 times a day.

136.

If you shuffle a deck of cards properly, it's more than likely the exact order of the cards you get has never been seen before.

137.

Only four words in the English language end in "dous"- tremendous, horrendous, stupendous, hazardous.

138.

One single teaspoon of honey represents

the lifes work of 12 bees.

139.

Honey is the only food that does not spoil.

140.

It is impossible for you to tickle yourself.

141.

Venus is the only planet

that rotates clockwise around the sun.

142.

To escape the grip of a crocodile's jaw, push your
thumbs into its eyeballs and it let you go instantly.

143.

The praying mantis is the only insect that can turn its head.

144.

There are 269 steps to the top of the Leaning Tower of Pisa.

145.

Pearls melt in vinegar.

146.

If you are ever being chased by a crocodile or alligator on land run in a zig zag manner. While they are fast they are not agile and this will help you gain ground away from them.

147.

There are 41,806 languages spoken in the world today.

148.

The top five languages spoken in the world are 1. Chinese 2. Spanish. 3. English 4. Hindi 5. Arabic

149.

In Disney's movie Fantasia,

the sorcerer's name is "Yensid,"

Disney spelt backwards.

150.

Plants grow faster when music

is played around them.

151.

Trees speak to each other by sending

signals to each other through their roots.

152.

Up to one billion birds die a year from

smashing into windows.

153.

Singing in a group boosts moral.

154.

Women hiccup less than men.

155.

The average person spends 10 hours a day online.

156.

An electric eel can produce a shock of 600 volts.

That's enough to knock a horse off its feet.

157.

A rhinoceros' horn is made of compacted hair.

158.

An octopus has three hearts.

159.

The stegosaurus dinosaur had a
brain the size of a walnut.

160.

There are more plastic flamingos
in the United States than real ones.

161.

Zebra stripes are a natural bug repellant.

162.

Dogs can make around ten vocal sounds.

163.

Cats can make more than 100 vocal sounds.

164.

Walruses turn pink if they lay
out in the sun for too long.

165.

Orang-utans protect their territory by burping loudly to warn off intruders.

166.

A dolphin can hear sounds up to 24 km (15 miles) away.

167.

Pteronophobia is the fear of being tickled by feathers.

168.

The longest human nose belonged to Thomas Wedders.

It measured 19cm (7.5 in)

He worked in a travelling show in the 1770's.

(People said he had a nose for the business).

169.

Earth is 4.543 billion years old.

170.

The average person spends three years
of their life on the toilet.

171.

One bat can eat 1000 mosquitoes
in a single hour.

172.

The average lead pencil can be used to draw a line
56 km long (35 miles) or to write
approximately 50,000 English words.

173.

In one year your heart beats around
42,048,000 times.

175.

The Empire State Building consists
of more than ten million bricks.

176.

A car travelling a 160km (100 miles) per hour
would take more than 29 million years
to reach the nearest star beyond the sun.

177.

In the average lifetime it is estimated a person
will breathe in around 20 kg(44lb) of dust.

178.

You blink over ten million times a year.

179.

The wheelbarrow was invented in China.

180.

A pregnant goldfish is called a twit.

181.

Red is the first color a baby sees.

182.

White is the safest car color.

183.

The most popular color in the world is blue.

184.

20% of the world's population speaks English.

185.

Green is the rarest human eye color.

186.

Outer space begins 80 km (50 miles) above the Earth.

187.

When awake, cats spend up to 30% of their time grooming.

188.

The Pacific Ocean is not as salty as the Atlantic Ocean.

189.

Diamonds are flammable.

190.

People started keeping ferrets as pets 500 years before they began keeping cats

191.

Most farts occur at night.

192.

Studies suggest that children ask around 73 questions every day.

193.

The South Pole is colder than the North Pole.

194.

Snakes can't blink.

195.

The temperature of the earth's core is around 7,500 Kelvin,

which is hotter than the surface of the sun.

196.

On planet Neptune days are 16 hours long.

197.

A typical cough travels at 60 mph.

198.
A typical sneeze travels at around 100 mph.

199.
Your brain is made up of 80% water.

200.
The tongue is the strongest muscle in the human body.

201.
The Queen owns all the unclaimed swans in England.

202.
The average time for plastic to decompose is 450 years.

203.
The average time for glass to decompose is 4,000.

204.

27,000 trees are cut down every day
to make toilet paper.

205.

The average person will spend 25 years asleep.

206.

The moon orbits the Earth every 27.32 days.

206.

The average person has 67 different species

of bacteria in their belly button.

207.

Elephants are pregnant for 22 months.

This is the longest period of gestation

of any land mammal.

208.

Black pepper is the most popular spice in the world.

209.

Candles burn better and last longer when they are frozen.

210.

It snows metal on planet Venus.

211.

Apes laugh when they're tickled.

212.

A "moonbow" is a rainbow that happens at night.

213.

Lobsters wee from their faces

214.

The oldest living tree in the world is in California. It is around 4,843 years old. The exact location of the tree is a secret.

215.

Unless food is mixed with saliva you can't taste it.

216.

The Hawaiian alphabet has 13 letters.

217.

The sentence "the quick brown fox jumps over the lazy dog," uses every letter of the English Alphabet.

218.

Only 3% of Earth's water is drinkable.

219.

Shakespeare invented over 1700 words. Many of the words we used today were first recorded in Shakespeare's writings including luggage, caked, buzzer and elbow.

220.

The word 'queueing' is the only English word with five consecutive vowels?

221.

If you sneeze too hard you could fracture a rib.

222.

It is impossible to sneeze with your eyes open.

223.

Whales can swallow half a million calories in a single mouthful.

224.

The fart bubble of a Blue Whale is so huge it could enclose a horse.

225.

The longest street in the world is Yonge Street in Toronto Canada measuring 1,178 miles or 1,895 km.

226.

If you add up all the numbers from 1-100 consecutively the total is 5050.

227.

The Taj Mahal in India is made entirely of marble.

228.

Only around 10 % of the population

can touch their nose and chin with their tongue.

229.

A shark's big fierce teeth aren't really teeth,

they're scales, like the scales on

the outside of most fish.

230.

Koala bears are not bears.

They are marsupials.

231.

Armadillos can walk under water.

232.

There are more than 1,000 kinds

of bats in the world.

233.

A horse has 18 more bones than a human.

A horse has 278, compared with

260 in an adult human.

234.

Guinea pigs aren't pigs at all but rodents, like rats.

Some people think they got their name because

they squeal like pigs.

235.

A gold fish will lose it's color if

it is not exposed to enough light.

236.

Lots of starfish have two tummies,

one inside that does most of the work,

and a second they can push outside

their mouth to trap big chunks of food.

237.

Wasps can get drunk from drinking
strong flower nectar.

They can even get so drunk that they fall down.

238.

Queen termites, can have 6,000 babies a day.

239.

Fleas can jump up to 150 times their height.

This is like a human jumping 1,000 feet in the air

or as high as 53 giraffes stacked

up on top of each other.

240.

A snail can have about 25,000 teeth.

241.

A cockroach can hold its breath for 40 minutes

and survive underwater for half an hour.

242.

Caterpillars have about 4,000 muscles.

People have 629.

243.

There was once a dinosaur on earth

known as eohippus (e-oh-hip-us)

that was a prehistoric horse

the size of a small dog.

244.

A triceratops dinosaur gets its name because

it has three horns on top

of its head and "tri" means three.

245.

The largest flying insect ever was a

prehistoric dragonfly.

It was about the same side as a tricycle

and had a wingspan of nearly 3 ft (0.91m).

246.

Cockroaches have lived on earth since dinosaur times, around 300 million years.

247.

Asparagus contains a chemical called methanethiol, which smells like rotten eggs.

248.

Almonds and peaches are in same plant family

249.

One dairy cow makes about 200,000 glasses of milk in her lifetime.

250.

There are about 20,000-25,000 grains of sugar in a teaspoonful

251.

A camel's hump is made of fat.

252.

Sugar comes from two kinds of plants, sugar beets, which grow underground like potatoes, and sugar cane, which is like thick, tall grass.

253.

Raisins are dried up grapes

254.

Prunes are dried up plums.

255.

The largest watermelon in the world weighed 262 pounds, the size of a football player.

256.

Tofu is made from a bean that grows on a plant.

257.

Red bananas have reddish-purple skin
and can taste like strawberries.

258.

If you drove to the sun in a car going
55 miles per hour (88km),
it would take you about 193 years to get there.

259.

There's a kind of star named White Dwarf,
and another named Red Giant.

260.

On a very clear night you may be able
to see around 2,000 stars in the sky.

261.

Alaska has more earthquakes than California.

262.

Neil Armstrong was the first man
to walk on the moon in 1969.

263.

You can still see traces of Neil Armstrong's
footprints on the moon's surface.
This is because there is no wind on the moon.

264.

It is believed that there are between
200-400 billion stars
in the Milky Way galaxy.

265.

It takes the light from the Sun
about 8 minutes to reach Earth.

266.

The Great Barrier Reef in Australia
is the largest living structure on Earth.

267.

The Great Barrier Reef spans about
2,000 kilometres and is made up of coral
islands and reefs.

268.

It takes 90 days for one drop of water
to travel the Mississippi River.

269.

The Mariana Trench is the deepest
part of the ocean.

270.

Mount Everest could fit inside
the Mariana Trench.

271.

In the Mariana Trench there is a section called The Challenger Deep, which is currently the deepest known point of the seabed.

272.

The Dead Sea has 8 to 9 times more salt than other oceans and seas of the world.

273.

It is harder to drown in the Dead Sea.
The increase in salt means humans are more buoyant in the Dead Sea.
It is harder to drown when you are floating on the surface.

274.

There are 840 different languages spoken in Papua New Guinea.

275.

Frazer Island in Australia is the world's largest island made of sand.

276.

Mawsynram in India is the wettest place on earth.

277.

There are no mosquitoes in Iceland. No one is sure why.

278.

The Moon reflects light from the Sun. During the night, the moon reflects the light from the Sun which is why we can see it so clearly.

279.

For a rocket to get into orbit around Earth, it needs to travel 17,600 miles per hour!

280.

If you wanted to go even further into space,

out of Earth's gravity,

you would need to travel up to

25,000 miles per hour!

281.

The temperature of space is
minus 270.45 Celsius

282.

Russian Valery Polyakov holds the record for

the longest time an astronaut has spent in space.

He was in space for 437 days!

283.

Valery Polyakov was up in space from

January 1994 until March 1995.

He orbited the Earth 7,000 times, spending his

days doing experiments and scientific research.

284.

Sharks don't have bones they have cartilage.

285.

The tentacles of the giant Arctic jellyfish

can grow to 120 feet.(36.5 m)

That's as long as 100 small cars lined up

bumper to bumper!

286.

Some baby elephants suck their trunks

for comfort like humans suck their thumbs.

287.

Elephants hug trunks to say hello.

288.

There are more than 1,000 kinds of bats in the world.

289.

Ears of corn generally have an even

number of rows, which is usually 16.

290.

Scientists in Germany have worked out a way to turn peanut butter into diamonds.

291.

White chocolate doesn't actually contain

any real chocolate.

292.

Antartica is the windiest place on Earth.

293.

Some gummy candies are coated with

carnauba wax. This is the same wax used on cars

to make them shiny.

294.

Chili peppers contain a chemical

that tricks your mouth into "thinking" it's being

burned and that is why spicy food hurts so much.

295.

Processed cheese was invented in Switzerland.
Walter Gerber and Fritz Stettler invented
processed cheese in Switzerland in 1911
to improve its shelf-life
before it was shipped overseas.

296.

The vanilla flavoring in some foods
comes from a secretion made by beavers.

297.

Figs aren't fruits, they're flowers.

298.

Jelly beans and other glazed candies
are commonly coated in
hardened insect secretions
known as shellac.

299.

Shellac is a processed and hardened resin secreted by the female bug called "Kerria lacca," which can be found in India and Thailand.

300.

Humans can lose up to a litre of fluid a night by sweating and exhaling when snoring.

301.

The membranes in your nasal passages can produce up to seven litres of snot a week!

302.

Charles Osborne of Iowa had the hiccups for 68 years. He hiccuped from 1922-1990.

303.

Human farts can enter the atmosphere at around seven miles per hour.

304.

Humans fart enough gas in one day to fill a party balloon.

305.

Humans lose an entire outer layer of skin In around two to four weeks, roughly shedding 50 million cells a day.

306.

A scientist who studies farts is called a flatologist.

307.

Scientists have found mobile phones carry more bacteria than toilet seats.

308.

The Romans sometimes used powdered mouse brains as toothpaste.

309.

The most germ-ridden item

in the home is the kitchen sponge.

310.

More human twins are being born now

than ever before.

311.

Bats sing love songs.

312.

We are born knowing how to smile.

We do not have to learn it.

313.

Your thumb doesn't make a sound when

you snap your fingers.

The sound you hear is actually created by

your middle finger hitting against your palm

314.

Your skin is your largest organ.

315.

Lachanophobia is the fear of vegetables

316.

The word "SWIMS" is still "SWIMS"

when turned upside down.

317.

Elephants can hear frequencies

20 times lower than humans.

318.

In seven hours an elephant can produce

a pile of poop that weighs

the same as one average fully grown person.

319.

It is estimated 61% of Americans regularly

pee in the shower.

320.

There are no muscles in your fingers.

Bones and tendons do all the hard work.

321.

Your intestine is four times as long as you are.

322.

The Bleeding Tooth Fungus is a type

of fungus mushroom that oozes

bright red gobules of fluid.

323.

The corpse flower smells like rotting flesh.

It can grow up to ten feet tall.

324.

Koalas feed their baby koala's poop!

This helps them to digest Eucalyptus leaves

which is the only food they eat.

325.

The hag fish when under threat
will shoot snotty mucus at their attacker.

326.

The hairy frog, also known as the horror frog,

is able to break its own toes to

expose super sharp, claw-style bones to defend

themselves against predators.

327.

Sea cucumbers can eject all of their intestines

in front of an attacker as a defence.

328.

There is a parasite called the cymothoa exigua,

that will attach to a fish's tongue, eat the tongue,

and then become the tongue!

329.

A group of jellyfish can be called a bloom,

a swarm or a smack.

330.

There is a beetle called,
Rebimbartia attenuate, that if it gets swallowed
by a frog, it can make the frog want
to poop and it will be pooped out alive.

331.

Jellyfish are older than dinosaurs!
There are fossils from over 500 million years ago,
and scientists believe that they might have even
been around for 700 million years, making
them hundreds of million years older than dinosaurs.

332.

Jellyfish don't have a brain, a heart or lungs.
They don't need lungs as they
absorb oxygen through their skin
They don't have a heart as they do not have blood.
Instead of a brain they use nerves .

333.

Waterspouts have been known to pick
small animals such as fish,
and have them 'rain down' somewhere else.

334.

In 2012, an entire village in Spain
won the lottery.
In the small rural village of Sodeto,
population 250, everyone had a ticket
and shared in the winnings except one person.

335.

Omphalophobia is the fear of belly buttons.

336.

The oldest person ever to have lived
(whose age could be authenticated),
was French woman named Jeanne Louise Calment,
who was 122 years old when she died in 1997.

337.

The original name for the search engine Google was BackRub.

338.

It was renamed Google after the word googol was misspelt.

339.

Googol is the number one followed by 100 zeros.

340.

The platypus doesn't have a stomach. Their esophagus goes straight to their intestines.

341.

Some plants when under attack from insects can let out aromas that warn other plants and notify the attacking insects' predators.

342.

There are four buried lakes on Mars.

343.

The summit of Mount Everest is about the size of two Ping-Pong tables.

344.

Polar bears have black skin.

345.

Polar Bear fur is not white, it is see-through. It appears white as it reflects light.

346.

The man who designed the Pringles can Fred Bauer, had is ashes put in one and buried when he died.

347.

Before alarm clocks, there were alarm humans. The job of knocker upper, originated in Britain during the Industrial Revolution.
A knocker uppers job was to knock with a wooden stick on your door a couple of times. If you lived on a higher floor they sometimes s hot dried peas at your window to wake you.

348.

You could fit Rhode Island into Alaska 425 times.

349.

It would take 22.7 years to eat at every restaurant in New York City if you ate at a different one every day .

350.

The record for the most Ping Pong balls bounced against a wall with the mouth in 30 seconds is 34 times.

351.

There is a type of ant found only within a 14-block strip of New York City, known as ManhattAnt. Scientists believe it evolved due to isolation within the city and from an unhealthy diet of corn syrup.

352.

The world record for the

most ice cream scoops on a cone is 125 scoops.

The scoops balanced for 10 seconds.

353.

The world record for the most four leaf clovers

picked on one minute is 166.

354.

The world record for the most baked beans

eaten in 1 minute using chopsticks is 71 beans.

355.

The world record for the most toilet rolls balanced

on the head for 30 seconds is 12 rolls .

356.

The world record for keeping two balloons in the air is 1 minute and 9 seconds.

357.

The world record for the most plastic bottle caps stacked into a tower in one minute is 43.

358.

The world record for the most t-shirts worn at once is 260.

359.

The world record for the most spoons balanced on a face at one time is 31 spoons balanced for 5 seconds.

360.

The world record for the longest daisy chain is 2.12km (1.21 miles)

361.

Only 1% of the world's population is ambidextrous. Meaning they can use their right and left hand with equal skill.

362.

The world record for the quickest time to eat a jam donut without using hands is 11.41 seconds

363.

Less than 2% of people have red hair.

364.

In 2020 scientists found the first frog fossil in Antarctica. The frog lived around 90 million years ago, when Antarctica was a thriving rainforest before it froze.

365.

Hugs make you healthier.
Hugging someone for 20 seconds or longer releases a hormone called oxytocin. This hormone has been shown to boost the immune system, reduce stress and increase heart health.

CONGRATULATIONS!

365 AWESOME, RANDOM USELESS FACTS KNOWLEDGE AWARD

to

Signed:

Date:

There is no such thing as useless knowledge. You never know what door it's going to open up for you.

Benjamin Carson

Record your own list of random useless facts :

LOOK OUT FOR OTHER
ACTIVITY JAM BOOKS

Printed in Great Britain
by Amazon

81985191R00050